Don Koestner

American Impressionist

Don Koestner at the mouth of the Beaver River, Lake Superior, 1997.

Don Koestner

American Impressionist

Project organized and paintings selected by Michael Coyle and Annette LeSueur

Edited by William Hakala

Stone Arch Books

Books may be ordered from: koestner@fastmail.fm

Produced and published by Stone Arch Books, Afton, Minnesota
Book concept and project direction by Michael Coyle and Annette LeSueur
Graphic design and layout by Victoria Hakala
Edited by William Hakala

Printed by Service Printers, Duluth, Minnesota
Bound by Midwest Editions, Inc., Minneapolis, Minnesota

Library of Congress Control Number: 2005908826
ISBN 0-9773377-0-7

Front cover painting: *Beaver River Mouth* by Don Koestner, 2002, oil on canvas, 24 x 36 inches
Back cover photo: Koestner home and studio, North Shore

Photography credits:
Don Butterfield: Don Koestner near Silver Bay (page 128)
Richard Colburn: Don Koestner, Beaver River (page *ii*)
Bo Hakala: Koestner studio (pages 129, 132, 133)
Fern Koestner: portrait of the artist (page 124)
Jean Moline: Don Koestner grinding pigment (page 136)
Danielle Steele: Don and Fern Koestner at home on Lake Superior (page *x*); Don Koestner and studio (page 130); Koestner home on the North Shore (back cover)
James Whiting: Don Koestner, North Shore (page 139)

To Fern

June 1, 1934 – May 12, 2004

Without her support and enthusiasm this publishing project would not have become a reality.

Contents

Foreword *ix*
Michael Coyle

Introduction *xi*
Annette LeSueur

An Artist's Life 1
William Hakala

Gallery of Landscape Paintings 15

Gallery of Still Lifes and Portraits 111

Landscape Painting: The Artist's Perspective 121
Don Koestner

Painting Notes 124
Don Koestner (Compiled by Annette LeSueur)

Foreword

This book has been a dream of mine for a number of years, growing out of a desire to acquaint more people with the art of Don Koestner. Don is a master of impressionist painting, and landscape painting the most prominent expression of his talent.

I felt that an overview of Don's work would be an important record for connoisseurs and artists alike. When I first decided to pursue this project I approached Annette LeSueur. Our intentions were simple. We wanted to present a volume of reproductions of Don's art and include a short biography and some technical information for those interested. After discussing the book idea, we approached Don and his wife Fern and got their consent.

Don has an enormous body of work that represents some fifty-five years of painting. After selecting the desired paintings, Fern (who had kept a complete sales record) contacted clients and patrons to ask them to loan us their artwork for reproduction. This proved to be an enormous task because we had to collect a large number of paintings throughout the state of Minnesota, plus photo reproductions from across the United States.

This major publishing effort would not have been possible without the assistance of many people. Frederic Petters and Roger Hamm painstakingly photographed the artwork during a number of long sessions. Jeff Frey Photography, Inc. and Custom Photo Lab of Duluth provided digital reproductions and color transparencies of the paintings Don had in his studio. PQ Digital in Hopkins made photo reproductions and transferred images to disk.

Seven additional photographers provided their cooperation: Ron Butterfield, Richard Colburn, Bo Hakala, Fern Koestner, Jean Moline, Danielle Steele, and James Whiting photographed Don Koestner on location and at home.

We are grateful to the many owners of Don's art who loaned us their treasured paintings. The volunteers who collected the paintings for the photo sessions worked incredibly hard to insure that all of the artwork was safely transported to and from the photographers' studios. Annette and I thank them all for their participation: Roger Tonsager, Lou Stoffle, Paul Welshons, Russell Saulon, Wayne Howell, Brian Lewis, Rachael Lungstrom, Liane Buechler, Julie Hartranft, Danielle Steele, Rhett Roberts, Pat and Ron Allar, and Doug Morrissette.

We also thank the following people for volunteering their help: Stephen Gjertson for his consulting on the project; Barb Coyle for her advice in producing our layout mock-up; Julie Hartranft for agreeing to distribute books; Pat Allar for typing much of the text; Gary Christensen for his 1992 interview of Don Koestner in the *Classical Realism Quarterly*; Sean Coyle and Lohr Hathaway for inspiration; Rachael Lungstrom, Russell Saulon, and Frank and Julie Hartranft for help in organizing the photography project; Vicky Hakala for graphic design, final layout and production; Bill Hakala for writing and editing. (Bill Hakala is writing a comprehensive biography of Don Koestner,

A *Way of Living*, for future publication. Inquiries can be sent to Stone Arch Books, P. O. Box 250, Afton, MN 55001.)

Finally, we pay special tribute to Fern Koestner for her role in producing this book. Fern died in the midst of this project after a sudden illness. She was a driving force and we all grieve that she is not with us to celebrate this publication. She would have been immensely proud and excited to see this book become a reality.

—Michael Coyle

Fern and Don Koestner, 2003

Fern reviews slides for book project.

Introduction

Why a book about Don Koestner? Why is he so profoundly important to me, and why do I think he is so important to the world? The answers come on many levels.

First, his paintings of nature have literally taught me to see nature. I have often looked at a Koestner landscape with surprise and wonder. His paintings are always faithful and true; more faithful and true in my opinion than those of any other landscape painter. I remember seeing a particular painting with extraordinary light sky values and thinking, no, those values are too light. No sooner had I passed this judgment, however, than I began to notice the same exact sky values in nature and was forced to amend my opinion. To really see nature is one of the most important gifts I have received from anyone.

Second, Don has an amazing visual memory. He can glimpse the moment during a storm when the lighting is most dramatic or watch the subtle colors during a sunrise, hold them in his mind and then reproduce them on canvas with all the drama and power that were available to the rest of us only for a fleeting moment in time. He even seems to capture the temperature of the day. Because of his visual memory, Don's paintings provide a record of some of the most sublime moments of nature in paint. For patrons of his work, to own such a record is beyond price.

Third, Don is without guile. In our twenty-seven year association I have come to know him as a gentle, unassuming, and completely genuine person with a subtle sense of humor. I experience the integrity of Don in a Don Koestner painting. I like how I feel when I see his paintings. Don once told me he didn't believe in chance. Rather, he created opportunities with deliberate choices, not the least of which was his choice of a wonderful wife and partner and their decision to live in the wilds of nature on the north shore of Lake Superior in Minnesota.

Fourth, because of the new standard Don has set for landscape painting, he has made a vital contribution to the craft and method of landscape painting. Don has been active all his life in encouraging young landscape painters. He has shared freely what he has learned in a lifetime of study.

This book attempts to give a sense of Don's life, an accurate account of his many paintings, and a description of his craft and working methods. We hope this information will be useful in the training of future landscape painters.

—Annette LeSueur

Koestner 2001

An Artist's Life

Minnesota artist Don Koestner has inspired two generations of midwestern landscape painters—as an accomplished painter and teacher and as a model of discipline, perseverance, and resourcefulness. In the artist and the man is a unity of purpose.

Looking back on Don Koestner's fifty-five years of landscape painting, one cannot separate this traditional painter's faithful and often poetic renderings of nature from the virtues of his dawn-to-dusk work ethic and frugal lifestyle. His sense of mission has never flagged. In his eighties he finds painting as challenging and spiritually fulfilling as he did more than a half century ago: "It is what I do and who I am." He lives simply, sensibly, and fully and at his core is a happy man.

Donald Edgardine Koestner was born in Saint Paul on November 28, 1923, the second child of working-class parents. His sister, Lorraine, arrived four years earlier. Their mother, Frieda Umbreit, and father, John (Jack) Koestner, were of German ancestry. The family lived in West Saint Paul until the artist was ten.

In grade school, Koestner demonstrated a talent for drawing, and his teachers often praised him for his art. But his hardworking parents considered art an impractical activity and offered no encouragement, hoping he would outgrow the interest. In 1933, the family moved to south Minneapolis so Jack Koestner could be closer to his job at the Lake Street plant of Minneapolis-Moline Power Implement Company, a manufacturer of farm machinery.

Outgoing as a youngster, Don Koestner turned inward in adolescence. He was small in stature, had a slight speech defect, and suffered frequent headaches because of a vision impairment. It continued uncorrected until he had completed high school and had an eye exam as part of applying for a job. In high school, despite his high scores on intelligence tests, he took easy courses, studied little, and withdrew from most social and sports activities. During this period, the artist says, he became acutely aware of the natural world, observing such things as "the play of light and shade on trees, and the way cumulus clouds have flat bottoms."

Koestner spent part of his summer vacations on an uncle's small farm near Becker, in Sherburne County. He enjoyed the simplicity of 1930s rural life, where neighbors helped each other with plowing and harvesting. His uncle farmed with horses and lived in a home without electricity and indoor plumbing. Although Koestner was too timid to do sketches on these visits—his art interest was understood no more there than at home—he worked from memory later to produce pastels and watercolors of what he saw. From that early experience grew a lifelong feeling for the beauty of midwestern farmlands. From his uncle he learned lessons in simple living that were useful later in his life.

As a teenager, Koestner felt out of step with mainstream art.

Opposite: *Beaver River Mouth,* 2001, 24 x 36 in.

One art teacher, trying to coax expressiveness from her students, labeled his drawings "too photographic." He found his best drawing instruction in Watson-Guptill how-to books. Equipped with sketchpad, pencil, and *How to Draw Trees*, he ventured out on his Montgomery Ward bicycle to draw trees along the Mississippi River bluffs near his home. He drew carefully, often returning to the same place to work more on his drawing.

During his last two years of high school, Koestner's art teacher helped him obtain scholarships to attend Saturday classes at the Minneapolis School of Art (MSA). Hungry for instruction, he enjoyed the classes but sometimes argued with his instructor about the merits of modern artworks, reproductions of which she often showed the class. Koestner increasingly felt out of step with the direction that art and art education had taken. "My sole interest then—as now," he says, "was to record the beauties of nature."

Koestner graduated from high school in the spring of 1941—six months before Japan's attack on Pearl Harbor—and received a partial scholarship for a six-week landscape painting class at MSA. This was the artist's first experience with the medium of oil, and during the daily three-hour morning class, the students worked on location doing sixteen-by-twenty-inch paintings. When his teacher recommended a book on the technical aspects of oil painting, he bought a copy. Max Doerner's *The Materials of the Artist and Their Use in Painting*, published in 1934, became a Koestner bible.

Once Koestner completed the spring painting class, his father insisted that he give up his "art stuff" and get a job. He found work with the Twin City Rapid Transit Streetcar Company as a car checker, recording streetcar arrival times and passenger counts at various intersections. He worked there and with several other companies until he was drafted in 1943. Military service in World War II halted his plans to become an artist, but he decided while on a troop ship headed for North Africa that if he survived the war he would enter art school. Of his army experience—he was discharged in 1946 with the rank of sergeant—he says, "It was basically a good thing for me, and I had some interesting travels." The young soldier was in transit three months before reaching his assigned base in southeastern China. En route he rode French boxcars from Casablanca to Oran through the Atlas Mountains of Algeria, left Oran for Bombay on a British troop ship, and after two weeks in Bombay rode a train to Calcutta. From there he traveled by train and riverboat to a port in northern India, from which he was flown over the Himalayas to China. Still timid about drawing in public, he did little while in the army. He bought a sketchbook in Bombay, however, and made a few drawings from memory while lying in his bunk at night. He became a draftsman for the U.S. Army Air Forces unit to which he was finally assigned, and he remained in China until the end of the war.

The G.I. Bill of Rights made Koestner's resolution to study art an achievable goal, and in September 1946 he enrolled at the Minneapolis School of Art. There he made several lifelong friends among fellow students. One was Richard Lack, who with several others shared an interest in traditional art. Not finding

Opposite: *Passing Showers, Lake Superior,* 1980, 30 x 36 in.

at MSA the kind of training in drawing and painting they sought, the students began to teach themselves. Koestner, always fascinated by the technical aspects of painting, discovered a book, Jacques Maroger's *The Secret Formulas and Techniques of the Masters*, in the museum library. He adopted many of the French art restorer's practices in 1949 and continues them today.

Koestner supplemented his painting knowledge by studying museum collections, traveling to the Windy City as often as he could to visit the Art Institute of Chicago. In the summer of 1948 he and art-school friend Cliff Moen took a three-month, 6,000-mile tour of the South and the East in Moen's Model A Ford. The two adventurers—both veterans—slept in pup tents, and bathed in ponds and rivers. In addition to doing pen and wash sketches nearly every day, they visited museums in Saint Louis, New Orleans, Washington, Philadelphia, and New York, as well as cities in Florida. The next summer Koestner visited the Art Institute of Chicago twice and on one of those trips also visited museums in Toledo and Detroit.

Awarded a $400 travel-and-study scholarship upon his graduation from art school in 1950, Koestner made another trip east. He spent a week each in Boston, New York, and Washington, with stops at museums in other cities along the way. These early trips contributed greatly to his knowledge and appreciation of painting.

Koestner pondered the artist's dilemma of how to make a living with his art and determined not to become a weekend painter who worked the rest of the week in an office or factory. He knew he had years of learning ahead to master his craft but looked for a way to paint "on as full a schedule as possible." A few weeks before Koestner's graduation that spring and several months before his trip east, a student friend lent him her copy of Henry David Thoreau's *Walden*. The book made an immediate and powerful impression on him. Thoreau's famous counsel to "simplify, simplify" gave Koestner a beacon to follow. At graduation, he told the young woman who had lent him her book, "Next year at this time I'll be living in a cabin in the woods."

Inspired by Thoreau's example and enabled by a $500 commission for a Minneapolis church mural that summer, Koestner bought four-and-a-half acres of land on a bluff overlooking the Mississippi River near Hastings, thirty miles south of the Twin Cities. To save money for cabin-building the following spring, he found a night job driving a cab. With characteristic faith in his instincts, the artist, with no idea of how he would support himself during construction, trusted that "things will work out." They did. In April, when Koestner was about to quit his job, the cab-company owner asked him to continue working on weekends. Thus in the summer of 1951 the artist spent five days each week building his cabin and on Saturdays and Sundays drove a cab.

Koestner built his fourteen-by-twenty-two-foot cabin with drift lumber salvaged from sandbars in the river and a $40-buys-all offer of framing and windows from a demolished fraternity house on the University of Minnesota campus. His total cash outlay for construction materials and secondhand furnishings

Opposite: *Summer Sunset,* 1983, 37 x 44 in.

was less than $300. Though raised in the city, he learned to heat with a woodstove, cut and stockpile wood, and collect water from the river for cooking and bathing (in the winter chopping through ice with an ax). Mechanically inclined, he did his own car maintenance on a succession of old, high-mileage cars, and he lived on his $15 weekend earnings. Beginning that fall, he painted five days a week.

In the winter of 1953–54, Koestner returned to full-time cab driving to save money for a trip to Europe with Cliff Moen, his companion on the 1948 trip. In early April they took a steamship from Quebec to Le Havre, France. After buying a bicycle, Koestner had $200 with which to spend four months in Europe. The two artists did sketches as they biked and camped through France and parts of Italy, Austria, and Germany, visiting art museums along their route. They sold their bikes in Frankfurt and hitchhiked north through Belgium and Holland, ferried across the channel, and spent a week in London before leaving Liverpool for home.

Koestner was particularly impressed with oil landscape sketches he saw in Florence—oil sketches done in nature rather than in a studio—and pursued the same practice when he returned home in August. He also began doing larger oil paintings on location.

Richard Lack returned to Minneapolis in 1957 from his studies in Boston with artist R. H. Ives Gammell and shared with Koestner the knowledge he had acquired. About that time, a group of women from Hastings asked Koestner to be their painting instructor. He agreed, and in 1959 a similar group invited him to teach in Red Wing, a town thirty miles downriver. The income from teaching these two groups surpassed his average while cab driving, so he gave up that job.

The Red Wing group held a one-man show for Koestner in December of 1959, forever after marking a milestone in his life. At the opening he met a young woman, Fern Bolin, who subsequently joined his evening class. He began courting her on February 29—Leap Year 1960—and on June 30 the two were married.

Anticipating marriage, Koestner made plans to modernize and enlarge his cabin. To finance the remodeling he took a job in May 1960 at Art Instruction Schools, a Minneapolis-based correspondence school where several of his artist friends worked. He spent evenings and weekends doing carpentry on the expansion of the cabin, but he hired out the cement, plumbing, and electrical work. After a year of working full time at Art Instruction, he cut back to a half-week schedule—the couple repaid their construction loan from a Hastings bank in six months—thus giving himself more time for painting.

Although originally inclined to paint only landscapes, Koestner discovered that he liked painting figures too. He did portraits to supplement his income, charging $15 for charcoals and $50 for oils.

Koestner was inspired by the Impressionist paintings he viewed at the Art Institute of Chicago and in other museum collections, and he began applying their broken-color method in his work in 1959. After their marriage, Fern sometimes modeled for paintings. Richard Lack persuaded him to do still life paintings as well. Koestner rendered many of these in broken color, using the “sight size” approach. This entailed placing

Autumn in the Midwest, 1990, 30 x 48 in.

Autumn Sunset, 1984, 29 x 46 in.

the canvas next to the subject painted and viewing subject and canvas side by side from ten or twelve feet. Koestner says, "The introduction of this method was Lack's major contribution to my knowledge of painting processes." Although he could not strictly apply the method to landscape painting because of the large scale of his outdoor subjects, Koestner thereafter placed his canvas in such a manner that he could view his subject and painting together with a minimum of eye movement.

The artist and his bride had honeymooned on the North Shore of Lake Superior in northeastern Minnesota, and in following years they vacationed in that area. In 1968 Koestner received a commission to paint a background diorama for an exhibit at the Goodhue County Historical Society Museum in Red Wing. With the prospect of a $2,000 fee, the Koestners decided to build a cabin-studio on the shore of Lake Superior —provided they could find affordable land. Although land prices were rapidly rising beyond his means, Koestner was able to buy two lots comprising one-and-one-half acres on a thirty-foot cliff overlooking the lake near the town of Silver Bay. The property's elevation and location on the lake were a painter's dream come true. He was particularly impressed with a massive stone arch formed by the big lake's waves, and it became a much-repeated subject in his work.

During his first years of living on the Mississippi River, Koestner had discovered that good lumber often washed up on the river's islands and banks, so in the fall of 1968 he again began collecting drift lumber for cabin building. (Providentially, a flood in the spring of 1969 sent an abundance of material downriver from the Twin Cities.) In June the artist quit his by-then-one-day-a-week Art Instruction job and with eight loads of salvaged lumber headed north with a borrowed trailer. With help for the first week from a young Hastings friend, he built a twelve-by-sixteen-foot cabin-studio in one month. Again, his cost for construction materials was less than $300.

By that summer the Koestners had a six-year-old son, Frederick, and a five-year-old daughter, Lorna. To more conventional parents, quitting a salaried job and building a cabin would have seemed irresponsible, but Fern agreed to the decision. Koestner recalls, "In our years of generally hand-to-mouth existence we adopted the phrase 'Oh, something will turn up,' and it always did whenever money got troublingly low." At the time, he was selling paintings for $200 to $300. The Hastings community staged several shows for him and provided patronage as well.

That fall, back home on the river after the summer of North Shore cabin-building, Fern obtained commissions for Don to do pastel portraits, mostly of children. He preferred to have his subjects pose, but he mostly worked from snapshots. "I charged only $30," he says, "but was able to secure enough commissions to provide grocery money for a year or two."

In 1970 Koestner began part-time teaching at the Minnesota Museum Art School in Saint Paul. The offer came unexpectedly in a phone call the night before the morning class was to begin. He accepted but felt insecure, having only limited experience in teaching amateur groups. "I slept little that night," he says, "but needn't have worried." He found the museum school was run casually, and his students were much like those he had taught previously. He taught a half-day drawing class the first season, then for the next four years a morning portrait-and-figure class and an afternoon still-life class. As his classes gained in popularity, he had the satisfaction of seeing students return each year and of watching their work progress.

At the end of the school year in 1975, the museum abruptly closed the school. About that time, Richard Lack moved his art school, Atelier Lack, into larger quarters in Minneapolis and offered Koestner the opportunity to teach an avocational class to help him pay the rent. Koestner's Saint Paul students were pleased to hear that their classes might continue in Minneapolis, so he began teaching once a week at Atelier Lack. This continued until 1985.

From 1970 until 1985 the Koestners spent summers and some school holidays on the North Shore and the rest of the year at their Hastings home. During those years Don became increasingly devoted to landscape. In addition to continuing with outdoor painting, he began doing larger canvases in the studio, working from outdoor oil sketches or from pencil drawings and a memory color sketch. When possible, he did both studio and outdoor work on the large canvas. He also discovered he could paint outdoors in winter by mixing a few drops of kerosene with the paint on his palette. Because of these factors he abandoned still-life painting and did fewer figure pieces, devoting most of his time to his real passion—landscape.

In the fall of 1985, their children grown, the Koestners decided to sell their Hastings home and convert their North Shore cabin into a year-round home. Those plans forged ahead even though Koestner had bypass surgery after a mild heart attack in November. Having recovered normal health, he spent the summer of 1986 helping with the remodeling and additions to the cabin.

At the time of his surgery Koestner was sixty-two years old. He applied for Social Security and retired from part-time teaching. Since then he has painted Lake Superior and its surrounding cliffs and forests with undiminished enthusiasm. He maintains a liking for the farm and river landscapes of the Mississippi Valley as well. When fall colors faded in the north, he and Fern traveled south for two or three weeks to extend his autumn painting opportunities in a landscape different from that of northern Minnesota. His habit has been to do oil sketches on these trips, and with some help from photographs and notes, turn them into larger paintings during the winter. He usually does a winter landscape or two. No longer wishing to do outdoor painting in the winter, Koestner often paints from windows of his home.

Over the years, this largely self-taught painter has developed his own style, and identifying specific influences in his paintings has become more difficult. He says, "I've been impressed with the work of a wide variety of painters, and several have had a definite influence." He names Hans Holbein the Younger as an influence while he was in art school, and he has a life-size seated self-portrait in which he strived to emulate the sixteenth-century German-born Swiss painter.

In landscape, Koestner's early influences were Camille Corot and other Barbizon painters, the Hudson River School painters, and George Inness.

Opposite: *The Birchwood Morning,* 1988, 30 x 40 in.

Koestner has employed the glazing techniques he admired in Inness, Thomas Moran, and J. M. W. Turner—combined with broken-color methods—in a number of his paintings. He gradually absorbed the Impressionist influence of Claude Monet and has followed Monet's practice of doing "series" paintings. Koestner made dozens of paintings of the stone arch on his shoreline before a severe storm destroyed it on November 1, 1995, and finds series paintings a logical course for an outdoor painter. While painting outdoors, he can observe the appearance of his subject change with the movement of the sun. "A couple of hours of time can give me a quite different picture of the same elements," he says. "Besides, I've long considered the light effect to be the main subject of my landscapes."

We live in a time of social and cultural upheaval, the outcome of which no one can foresee. What role the visual arts will play in this century is equally unfathomable, but there are signs that an interest in traditional art is growing. I have long felt that, in time, the painting of our era will be stacked up against that done in the past, and only work that has relevance to the human experience and that compares favorably in beauty and craftsmanship will last. If at such a time my art is deemed worthy to be kept, my expectations will have been met.

—Don Koestner, 2005

The artist's brightest light was extinguished on May 12, 2004, when Fern died of lung cancer—two weeks before her seventieth birthday. Her cancer had been detected only two months earlier. The couple was married forty-four years. Painting helped Koestner through this period. It is a powerful and deeply enriching focus—the center around which he lives his life.

In the fall of 2004, Koestner felt compelled to act on a plan that Fern and he had made to revisit the rolling bluff land that rises above the Mississippi River in northeastern Iowa. He had painted in the region many times before. The rural area's interlacing fields, pastures, and woods epitomize what one of the artist's favorite painters, George Inness, called "the civilized landscape." Koestner made the ten-hour drive to Guttenberg, Iowa, alone, stayed in the area ten days, and did oil sketches at three different sites. He spent much of that winter and following spring in his studio making large paintings from his sketches.

Koestner continues to live much as he has the past fifty-five years. On occasion this traditional painter expresses his disappointment that the modern-art establishment has excluded him and his colleagues from museum shows, galleries, and the art press. But he is philosophical about the absence of recognition: "I have had a good life, work that I love, and the time and freedom to do it. Adopting Thoreau as an early mentor, I have tried to live a simple life. For most of our years together, Fern and I lived considerably below what the government declares poverty level, but we did not feel deprived and did most of the things we wanted to. Although my work is not widely known, there were always enough people buying paintings to keep us financially afloat. That's been enough to satisfy me."

Looking back, Koestner says that too much has been written about aims in the visual arts and that he prefers that his work be judged solely on the viewer's reaction. The visual phenomena of nature continue to move him. He strives to recreate the impression a subject has made upon him, hoping to preserve a fleeting effect and transmit it to others.

—William Hakala

Gallery

Landscape Paintings

Autumn Leaves, 1994, 30 x 32 in.

Gold Point Rock, 2001, 29 x 31 in.

Backyard Moonlight, 1990, 28 x 26 in.

The Red Oak, 1994, 30 x 48 in.

The Old Orchard, c. 1960s, 18 x 24 in.

North Shore in Spring, 1997, 28 x 34 in.

Mississippi Valley, Autumn, 1981, 36 x 48 in.

North Shore Cliffs, c. 1970s, 24 x 30 in.

The Old Pine, c. 1970s, 18 x 10 in.

An Autumn Mosaic, 1998, 36 x 28 in.

Stone Arch, 1974, 36 x 24 in.

The Island Iced-in, 1994, 26 x 36 in.

Autumn, 1987, 30 x 44 in.

Autumn Birches, 1993, 32 x 26 in.

Autumn Oaks and Locust, 1997, 26 x 46 in.

Coon Valley, 1999, 24 x 60 in.

Early Morning Autumn, 1993, 36 x 48 in.

Oat Shocks, 1965, 14 x 20 in.

Clearing Up, 1992, 25 x 40 in.

An Autumn Oak, c. 1990s, 26 x 42 in.

A Fisherman's Relic, 1999, 24 x 30 in.

Beaver, 1996, 24 x 30 in.

Stone Arch, Cloudy Day, 1991, 32 x 34 in.

Stone Arch, Early Afternoon, 1992, 40 x 24 in.

Rainbow, c. 1970s, 31 x 37 in.

Winter Sunset, 1992, 22 x 28 in.

The Pre-Dawn Sky, 1999, 24 x 34 in.

Fisherman's Harbor, c. 1960s, 24 x 30 in.

Stone Arch, Partly Cloudy, 1992, 40 x 24 in.

Evening Light, 1987, 30 x 25 in.

At the Old Farm, 1996, 24 x 36 in.

The Old Homestead, 1980, 20 x 30 in.

Sunrise Through the Birches, 1989, 28 x 26 in.

Autumn Pastorale, 1993, 28 x 50 in.

Split Rock Lighthouse, 2002, 30 x 40 in.

A Winter Night, 1972, 20 x 24 in.

Spring Breakup, 1990, 14 x 18 in.

The Mississippi, 1980, 36 x 42 in.

Early October, 1981, 36 x 42 in.

Beaver River, Spring Runoff, 2002, 26 x 34 in.

An April Evening, 1983, 29 x 37 in.

October Farmland, 1994, 28 x 42 in.

The Old North Shore, 1999, 24 x 40 in.

A Rural Highway, 1996, 24 x 40 in.

Mississippi Valley Farm, 2003, 24 x 36 in.

Fireweed, 1971, 18 x 22 in.

Afternoon Light, 1987, 30 x 36 in.

January Sunshine, 1987, 30 x 32 in.

Evening Thunderheads, 1986, 37 x 50 in.

Minnesota Historical Society

Mouth of the Baptism River, c. 1970s, 30 x 36 in.

Sunrise After Snow, 1995, 26 x 32 in.

Winter Sunset, 1989, 24 x 32 in.

Stone Arch Spring Breakup, 1994, 40 x 24 in.

View of Shovel Point, 1988, 26 x 42 in.

September Farmland, 1982, 37 x 54 in.

Baptism River, Afternoon, 1972, 30 x 36 in.

Black Willow, 1992, 30 x 36 in.

The Old Shed, 1991, 24 x 30 in.

October Cornfields, 1995, 26 x 40 in.

Headland, 1996, 26 x 32 in.

Stone Arch, Summer Morning, 1995, 40 x 26 in.

Stone Arch, 1995, 32 x 26 in.

Northwoods, Autumn, 1998, 26 x 32 in.

Wisconsin Valley Farm, 1999, 28 x 34 in.

Aftermath of the Storm, 1988, 36 x 40 in.

View of the Islands, 1970, 22 x 28 in.

Late Hay Field, 1987, 14 x 18 in.

October Morning, 1999, 24 x 36 in.

A Morning Walk, 1995, 26 x 42 in.

October Morning Frost, 1997, 28 x 42 in.

Baptism River, Early Spring, 1995, 24 x 34 in.

In Dry Dock, 1984, 16 x 20 in.

The Hiawatha Valley, 1979, 30 x 48 in.

Lake Pepin, c. 1980s, 24 x 54 in.

The Delta Queen, 1975, 24 x 48 in.

Split Rock Lighthouse, 2004, 30 x 25 in.

After the Snowstorm, 1975, 30 x 36 in.

Prairie Sunrise, c. 1980s, 20 x 32 in.

Bob's Fish House, 2002, 20 x 30 in.

Autumn Asters, 2000, 24 x 40 in.

Old Machine Shed, c. 1960s, 12 x 16 in.

The Lone Farm, 1986, 30 x 46 in.

Morning Ground Fog, 1998, 24 x 48 in.

Minnesota Autumn, 1975, 24 x 30 in.

Quiet Evening, c. 1970s, 22 x 30 in.

Autumn in the Blue Ridge, 1989, 30 x 42 in.

The Old Farmstead, c. 1970s, 20 x 28 in.

Pond in May, 1984, 24 x 28 in.

February Moonrise, 1988, 36 x 22 in.

Snow and Moon, 1983, 25 x 37 in.

Moonrise, 1978, 20 x 28 in.

Morning in the Hills, 1980, 24 x 30 in.

In the Sawtooth Mountains, 1996, 32 x 48 in.

The Excursion Boat, 1995, 40 x 30 in.

Blossom Time, 1991, 24 x 30 in.

The Old Root Cellar, 1993, 20 x 30 in.

Upper Baptism River, c. 1970s, 24 x 30 in.

Moonlight, c. 1980s, 36 x 30 in.

Spring Storm on the Prairie, 2002, 32 x 50 in.

Saint Paul Cathedral, Sunrise, 1958, 24 x 30 in.

Mountain Elderberry, 1987, 20 x 24 in.

Water Lilies, 1994, 24 x 28 in.

Beaver Dam, 1996, 26 x 28 in.

Autumn Hills, 1993, 24 x 40 in.

Rattlesnake Bluff, c. 1980s, 20 x 30 in.

Stone Arch Nor'easter, 1995, 32 x 26 in.

The Remains of the Arch, 1996, 36 x 28 in.

Gallery

Still Lifes and Portraits

In the Pantry, 1970, 24 x 48 in.

Canning Time, 1969, 30 x 40 in.

Rosé Wine Decanter, 1969, 24 x 34 in.

Glass and Silver, 1978, 29 x 33 in.

The Babysitter, 1967, 20 x 16 in.

Lorna, 1967, 14 x 11 in.

Fern, 1960, 20 x 16 in.

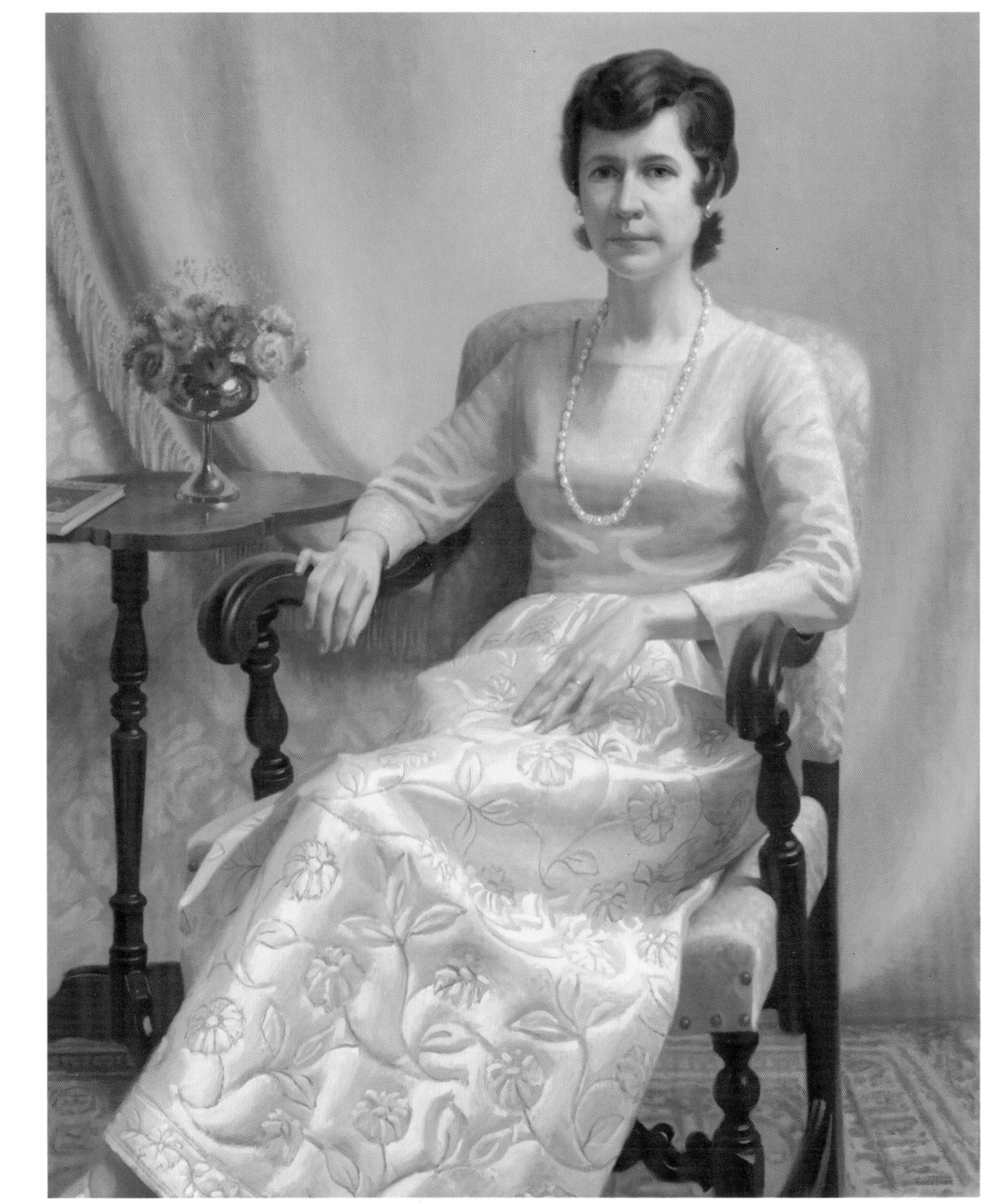

Portrait in Yellow, 1974, 48 x 36 in.

Self Portrait, 1950, 46 x 32 in.

Portrait of Mother, 1957, 26 x 20 in.

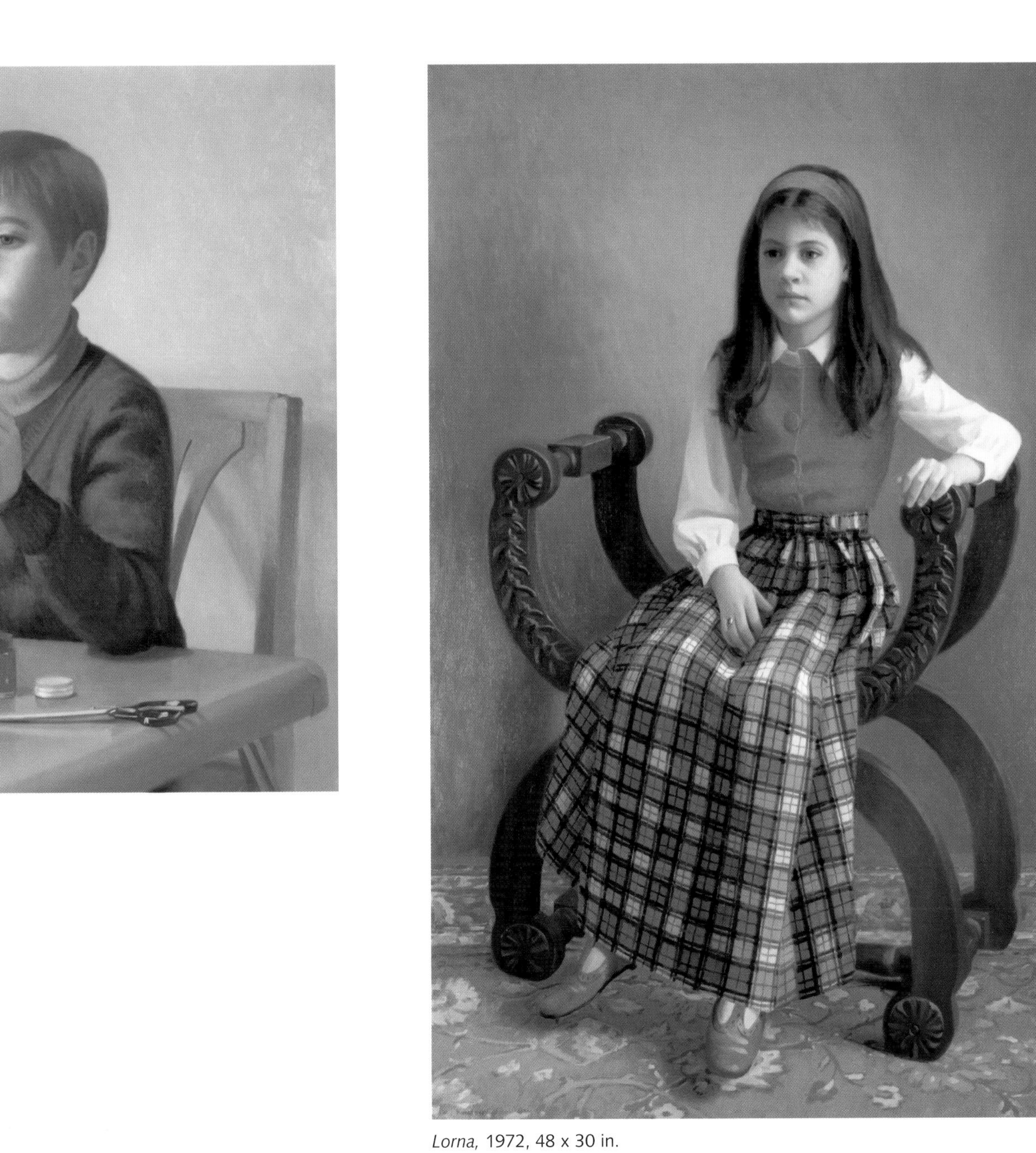

The Mayflower Model, 1974, 25 x 30 in.

Lorna, 1972, 48 x 30 in.

Don Koestner painting near Beaver Bay on the North Shore, 1991.

I've long considered the light effect to be the main subject of my landscapes.

—Don Koestner

Landscape Painting: The Artist's Perspective

For the artist addicted to landscape painting, there is perhaps no greater joy than working outdoors, attempting to capture some scene or effect in nature. As Emerson wrote, "In the presence of nature a wild delight runs through the man." I paint outdoors with an intensity and "wild delight" seldom approached in the studio.

Outdoor painting is not without its trials. In my opinion, wind is the greatest detriment. A large canvas acts like a sail in the wind, and my entire rig can be toppled by a sudden gust. Following the practice of earlier painters, I also use an umbrella to shade canvas and palette from the sun. Too much wind makes it impossible to keep it up. A slight breeze can be a blessing, however, for it keeps away many of the second curse of outdoor work—insects. There are a variety of creeping, crawling, and flying pests that can effectively distract a painter. Particular sections of the country have their unique pests. Much of my outdoor painting is done on the North Shore of Lake Superior, where the black fly is the prime enemy. This gnat-like creature not only bites exposed flesh, but crawls under collars and up pant legs where it continues to bite until apprehended.

To the hazards of wind and insects can be added the frustration of general weather conditions. A landscape painter has to have an eye out for the weather to an even greater extent than a farmer. I usually aim for a particular light or atmospheric effect and, when conditions are not precisely what I want, do as much preliminary work as possible. But once the painting is in its middle stages, work can proceed only when the weather is appropriate. A common occurrence is the persistence of cloudy days when the effect I'm after requires sunshine. Often I want to portray uncommon effects such as fog or passing cloud shadows, and have to wait days, weeks, or even years to get a sufficient number of correct days to complete a work. The problem is compounded in spring or fall, when seasonal changes afford, at best, a limited number of sessions on any single work. Landscape painters generally contrive to keep busy by having a number of works in progress simultaneously.

Preceding the Impressionists, and working during the same years with them, were other painters who chose to work on cloudy days, for then the light remains constant enough to allow a five- or six-hour painting session. The Impressionists reveled in sunshine and, consequently, were limited to a working session of only two or three hours because of the constantly changing light and shadow shapes.

In my north country, painting a winter landscape outside poses a particular challenge. Even with today's efficient cold-weather clothing, I put on as many layers as possible because the sub-zero cold penetrates much more when standing still for a couple of hours than when active. Here again, wind is the prime enemy. I have worked in temperatures as low as fifteen degrees below zero on calm days, but have had to give up at thirty degrees above because of the wind. I use snowshoes to get to my painting site, and stand on them while painting because they keep my boots from direct contact with the snow. Dressing warmly poses the risk of overheating while trekking long distances to the painting site. Because of this, I never go more than a quarter mile from car, house, or cabin. Cold temperatures also affect paint. I mix a few drops of kerosene with each mound of paint on the palette. Without this, the oil paint becomes too stiff for brushing.

In spite of the many problems and inconveniences I've cited, it is primarily for other reasons that artists forego direct work and turn to producing landscapes in the studio. Working out-of-doors, the tendency is to become overly influenced by the subject. Degas, who abhorred *plein-air* painting, referred to it as "losing consciousness in front of nature." Design is often less considered, and unity more difficult to achieve in a picture composed on the spot. It is difficult, if not impossible, to correct faulty underlying design (that combination of line and massing of dark and light shapes which adds up to a pleasing visual impression) out-of-doors. The problem of creating unity (that state in which a picture has a definite focus on a center of interest, and subordinate shapes, objects or colors retain their relative positions) can sometimes be better achieved by studio manipulation of color or value. For these reasons, artists have often composed and executed landscapes in the studio. Also, even in the artist's most objective attempt to interpret a scene, he filters it subjectively through his sensibility; this comes into play most fully in studio landscapes that often convey greater expressiveness. There, the raw material, drawings and/or color sketches done from nature can be organized. Time can be devoted to thumbnail sketches to determine the best canvas shape within which to organize the scene. The artist may decide to alter the placement of some elements, and eliminate others entirely. All these considerations are taken into account when one confronts a subject directly, but the spur of the moment decisions arrived at are sometimes adversely affected by nature's commanding presence. Another variation in working method is to begin the painting in the studio as I have described, and then transport it to the site for some direct work. I consider this method ideal if conditions allow, because painting from nature gives a certain authenticity to the work that studio productions sometimes lack.

Studio painting is absolutely necessary to depict the poignant, fleeting effects of nature that do not repeat themselves. Here, one generally does not have even the luxury of a color sketch from which to work. A sunset, rainbow, or particular cloud effect can disappear in less time than it takes to set up easel and palette. I particularly like to paint such moods of nature, and normally begin with a quick pencil sketch of shapes, along with some written notes on color. This is the most common method I have come to rely upon for capturing such phenomena. The method is not my invention. Sketchbooks of Turner, Moran, and many others contain such annotated drawings. At times I will make a color sketch as soon as possible afterwards, while my memory is fresh. Memory plays a large part in the production of any landscape done in the studio.

Quite often my studio landscapes represent a composite of observed elements. A beautiful cloud effect may be the motivation for a painting. After this is noted, I search for landscape components that would form an appropriate setting for that sky.

Reversing the process, I may stop on a trip perhaps to sketch an appealing view. Later, in the studio, I will search through accumulated sky sketches to find something that may be combined with the intended landscape. The experience of years of work and the consequent accumulation of knowledge is essential in producing a convincing finished picture of a fleeting effect. Such painting is not the province of the novice landscape artist, since it requires a combination of notes, memory, general knowledge, and invention.

In our age of the quick fix, many artists, faced with the trials and troubles of painting landscapes in the traditional manner, have turned to photography as their basic means of getting material for their work. (Here I am speaking of the use of photographs in producing works that fall under the category of traditional art, and not of the late avant-garde fashion of Photo Realism.) Photography can serve a legitimate and useful place in the production of paintings. Photos were used, more than is generally realized, by many fine painters in the nineteenth century. There is a difference, though, between the occasional use of a photographic aid by an accomplished painter and the almost total reliance on their use by many contemporary artists. Photography was used as an adjunct, rather than a substitute, for knowledge by the painters of the past. We have all been subjected to the photographic image that the public, and many artists, equate with visual reality. In fact, the eye perceives things differently from the way a camera records them. Looking at a tree, for instance, the eye sees a mass of color and value shapes, whereas the camera records every leaf. Furthermore, photos generally distort value, color, and perspective.

These considerations aside, my greatest objection to using photography to produce paintings lies in the area of the subjective motivation. Before I became deeply involved in landscape painting, I sometimes took photos of scenes or special effects as is commonly done today. I became aware, however, of the inability of the developed slide or print to evoke the feeling inherent in the subject—the impression that had prompted me to photograph it. The filtering of the subject through the mind is lost in the mechanical image of the photographic print. Even the quickest of pencil sketches and notation require more time, but they provide the artist with a much more lasting impression and memory of the thing observed than the flat image obtained by merely looking through the viewfinder and clicking the shutter. That subjective impression finds its way into a painting, and can be seen and appreciated by others.

Many present day representational paintings produced primarily by copying photographs are of an illustrative nature and not a development of the traditional art of painting as practiced for centuries in our Western culture. Examples of the former include much of the work in the popular categories of Wildlife Art or Southwest Art. In my opinion, true artistic expression, that elusive goal of the genuine painter, cannot be achieved without a direct and intense study of nature—a lifetime pursuit.

—Don Koestner

Painting Notes

The following observations and notes on how I work may suggest to some that my painting procedures are strict and unvarying. This is not the case. Every painting requires its own approach and method. The painter starts out with certain intentions and rules, but in the process the painting makes its own demands. That said, I trust that interested readers will find this information helpful.

—Don Koestner

Landscape Painting

▪ The idea that art, like fashion, must change every six months has led the Modernists into a sterile dead end. Art is an expression of a human being's reaction to life, and what has basic meaning in life does not change in spite of our technologies.

▪ I think dedicated landscape painters are born, not made, and they seek or respond to the proper influences.

▪ Among traditional artists, landscape painters have been somewhat a breed apart from those pursuing portrait, genre, or figure painting. Those artists whom we consider outstanding landscape painters have often been independent individuals who are less associated with academies, salons, or even teaching, than their contemporaries in other branches of painting.

▪ I advocate on-the-job training for landscape painters once

Don Koestner in his studio, 1988.

October Morning (color sketch), 1999, 12 x 18 in. (painting on page 75)

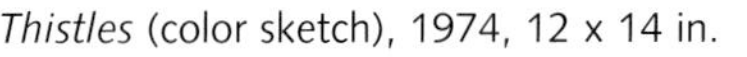

Thistles (color sketch), 1974, 12 x 14 in.

they have had basic training in drawing and painting. Working outdoors presents problems not encountered in the studio, which one learns to cope with only through personal experience. Those genuinely attracted to landscape painting will, I believe, find their own path.

▪ Outdoor painters sometimes find themselves in serious weather situations. Once, doing a color sketch at a scenic overlook, I was standing near a metal guardrail. It had clouded up and the wind was rising. Someone drove by and told me a bad thunderstorm was predicted for the area. I kept on painting but took down the metal rod that holds my umbrella rig and put it in the car. A few moments later I heard an explosion and the heavy metal guardrail twanged like a guitar string. Lightning had apparently hit it but I was unharmed. On my way back to the motel, I saw some beautiful cloud effects.

▪ When landscape painting, spectators are my least problem generally because I often paint in locations people don't frequent. When I have worked where there are lots of people, they have almost without exception been friendly and complimentary, or else have ignored me entirely.

Memory

Over the years I have developed a good visual and factual memory. In my adolescent years, I lived near the Mississippi River and liked watching paddle-wheel towboats. When a towboat whistled to enter the Ford Dam locks, I hopped on my bike and rode to a spot above them. There I observed and tried to remember the shapes and details of a particular boat, then biked home to do a pastel of it. When I began doing studio landscapes, I would note areas where my memory was deficient and observe these aspects on a subsequent visit. All my studio landscapes are now a combination of color sketches, pencil notes, general knowledge, memory, sometimes photos, and invention.

▪ Several of my paintings have been done from memory. Quite a number of my works are the result of seeing effects of sun and clouds while driving, and later doing memory sketches and color studies.

▪ At the start of a road trip to Tulsa, Oklahoma, to see a Moran exhibit, Fern and I went through the heaviest rainstorm we had ever experienced. It was like driving under water. We had passed through Saint Peter, Minnesota, before the storm came up. Finally we came out from under huge black clouds and when the sun came out, I knew I had the makings of a painting. At a restaurant that night, we learned that a tornado had hit Saint Peter a short time after we had passed through it. In the motel I made a memory pencil outline of the cloud masses. Back home, I did the memory color sketch from which my painting, *Spring Storm on the Prairie* (page 102), evolved.

▪ I sometimes combine elements I observe at different times. One such painting was planned as a sunset I had seen in 2001 while driving home from the Twin Cities, and then sketched

A Morning Walk (color sketch), 1994, 12 x 18 in. (painting on page 76)

View of Carlton Peak (color sketch), c. 1970s, 14 x 18 in.

Near Elba (color sketch), 1985, 12 x 18 in.

October Farmland (color sketch), 1993, 12 x 16 in. (painting on page 52)

from memory the next morning. In the foreground I painted four dark trees. The trees I utilized came from a 1960s drawing.

Influences

▪ During my years in art school I visited the museums of Chicago, Detroit, Toledo, Boston, New York, and Washington with the proceeds of school scholarships. These visits made me aware of my lack of knowledge about painting, but also imbued me with increased desire to emulate the great painters I had come to recognize and admire. Since those early trips, I have tried to visit good museums or a special show almost every year, and owe much of my development as a painter to such studies.

▪ Perhaps my greatest early influence was the work of George Inness, discovered in the Edward B. Butler collection of the Chicago Art Institute. Inness's paintings seemed magical to me in their evocative power while also retaining a look of truth. Though I have come to recognize his shortcomings, I still look to Inness as an ideal of expression in landscape painting.

▪ Artists who have influenced me in landscape painting include John Constable, Martin Johnson Heade, Childe Hassam, Claude Monet, George Inness, J. M. W. Turner, Jean-Baptiste Corot, Charles Daubigny, Thomas Moran, Frederick Church, Sanford Gifford, and Worthington Whitridge. I don't feel that I've gone beyond impressionism but I have combined it with other techniques such as glazing and scumbling, which I've picked up from Gifford, Turner, Moran, and Inness.

The River, October, 1978, 14 x 24 in.

Light Effects

▪ I am particularly interested in catching nature's fleeting effects. To this end, I have devoted my career to accumulating knowledge of nature, living within the context of the landscape I paint.

▪ I have often said the light effect is the real subject of many of my pictures. The most intriguing aspects of light, such as sunsets, fog, or the effect clouds have on the lake, never last long. I make attempts to cope with them in several different ways. At times I make a hasty pencil drawing with notes on color and value. I may later make a memory color sketch, and then make a studio picture from such material. If possible I'll paint the land elements on location. On occasion I've done a transient effect with a combination of a color sketch done on the spot and direct work on the picture whenever the phenomenon occurs again. *Aftermath of the Storm* (page 72) was done that way. I worked on it over a period of three years whenever the waves were high.

▪ My selection of subject comes from various sources, but most commonly from seeing what a particular light effect is doing to the landscape. Often, a light effect is my sole inspiration and then I search for appropriate landscape elements to put with the light effect.

▪ A prevalent notion is that the artist's sole motivation is to portray a particular scene with as photographic a verisimilitude as possible. But to the painter, the inspiration for the work may lie entirely in what the sun does to that scene at a particular time of day and season.

▪ I try to capture fleeting light effects because they are unique and the most poignant visual displays nature can present. In doing color sketches on trips, and often when scouting out a subject locally, I look for pleasing combinations of shapes: objects like buildings, for example, and striking light and dark contrasts. Then, while working on the same sketch several times, I am alert to any changes of lighting, sky, atmosphere, and shadow movement on the subject that I think would make the sketch and subsequently the final picture more interesting.

I can often make drastic changes, quite rapidly, to portray a more interesting mood or poignancy if the main structures and elements have already been established. On occasion I will entirely alter color and values of an older painting after seeing it at a later time—five, ten or even twenty years may have passed—and I can still make changes and improve upon it. I recently worked on one such painting. It is twenty-four-by-forty inches, looking down a road toward the sun, with brightly lit cumulus clouds. On a trip to Duluth I saw a similar sky and clouds that made me decide to re-do my old painting. I deepened the values of the sky and land elements but accented the

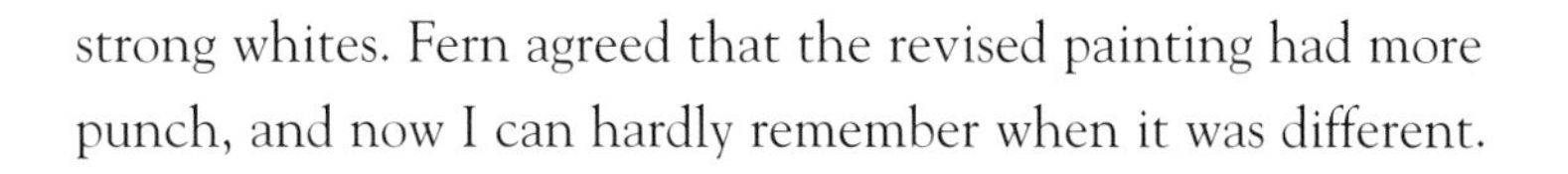

strong whites. Fern agreed that the revised painting had more punch, and now I can hardly remember when it was different.

▪ The biggest difference between outdoor painting and studio work is that outdoors the light source is constantly moving. This is particularly challenging when trying to capture a fleeting effect such as a sunset. Back lighting (the sun is in front of the artist) generally provides a larger window of opportunity than side lighting because the light remains constant longer with back lighting. I set up an umbrella when possible to shade the canvas and palette and wear a visor to protect my eyes from the sun.

Tools

▪ I have on hand all kinds of brushes, mostly hog bristles but also sables and synthetic blends, and in several different brands. I have sizes ranging from zero through twelve. I use the flat hog bristles mostly and also rounds, brights, and even the long-bristled egberts. I usually use sizes between four and ten.

▪ I mostly rely on my black mirror (a piece of plate glass painted black on the back), reducing glass, and looking upside down to see nature objectively. Outdoors, I often use a black mirror. I mostly hold the mirror up two feet or so away from the painting, shading it with a piece of cardboard if I'm painting toward the sun. I also carry a reducing glass and sometimes look through that into the black mirror, to reduce the painting and/or my subject way down. The black mirror is sometimes helpful in the studio but as I have a large regular mirror at the end of the studio, opposite the easel, I use that a lot.

▪ A black mirror is indispensable to seeing values correctly. I remember seeing the color of grass in a particular landscape scene and thinking its value was the same as the sky. Using the black mirror I was able to see their relationships better and saw that the grass was darker in value than the sky.

▪ Almost always the area of nature I plan to paint is quite large so I have to reduce it a lot on my canvas. Regarding that, however, I read that Corot often sat far back from the foreground he chose for his painting. This enabled him to do his sketch sight size. I think many of his fine small canvases of mountain villages were done like that. On several occasions I've done a small reverse landscape. I placed a five-by-seven-inch mirror next to a five-by-seven-inch panel on my easel and thus painted a sight-size five-by-seven-inch reversed image of the scene behind me; it's a good way to see values and colors. I did several paintings of Fern in that manner also.

▪ I have a collection of cardboard viewfinders proportioned to fit every painting shape I can think of. I have taped "cross hairs" in the openings to divide them into four quarters. I put the same cross lines on my canvas. This facilitates the initial layout of my chosen subject because I can easily see what elements appear in each quadrant. When looking for a place to paint I carry three or four of these finders in various shapes to help me choose my proposed painting. Often I use twelve-by-

Above: Work table in Koestner studio. Right: Don Koestner discusses his art, 2003.

A Rural Highway (color study), 1996, 12 x 18 in. (painting on page 54)

sixteen-inch or twelve-by-eighteen-inch canvases for the color sketches but on trips I have carried anything from square to twelve-by-twenty-four-inches. The "golden mean" size (approximately twelve-by-twenty-inches) is one I also like to use.

▪ I normally stand eighteen inches to two feet back from the easel but go back and forth a lot, too.

First steps

▪ I am not a painter to be watched. I avoid requests to give painting demonstrations because my paintings are built up slowly, the final painting containing many paint layers. (I also object to the implication that painting is a spectator sport.) I quite often begin a painting by putting down a color different than what will appear in the final work. One method I have used was introduced to me by an artist friend, Paul VanDemark. I have been calling it "separated broken color." It begins with using just one color at a time. I usually start with blue, laying out the picture with the proper values for each area as closely as they can initially be determined. After that layer has dried, a second layer, perhaps red, is laid on loosely leaving the blue exposed between strokes. A third layer of yellow would follow so all three primary colors are represented in their appropriate values. As with any intended procedure, each painting presents the artist with changes that are decided upon as the work progresses, so some of the broken color effect is lost in the end. Still, the finished painting contains a color vibration that enlivens the work. Examples of paintings produced in this manner are *North Shore Cliffs* (page 23) and *Stone Arch, Early Afternoon* (page 36).

▪ I lay out my palette as my first oil painting instructor taught me. Because I am left handed, the white goes on the upper left corner. Next to it the yellows: nickel titanium*, cadmium yellow primrose*, cadmium yellow medium*, and dark*. Then the reds: cadmium orange*, a bright red, vermillion*, cadmium red medium* and alizarin*. My blues are cobalt*, ultra marine*, thalo blue, viridian*, and emerald green—all down the right side—and occasionally black (of some kind) at the bottom right corner. (Asterisk means home-ground.) Thus: white, yellow, red, blue, green, black. I use a ten-and-three-fourths-by-sixteen-inch

View of Koestner studio with north-facing window and skylight, 2001.

palette. Values are mixed on the palette first but most color mixing is done on the canvas.

- Whenever possible, I shade my canvas with an umbrella but there are times when I stand on rock (or even hard-packed ground) and have no place to push my umbrella rod in and of course the wind is often too strong for the umbrella to stay up. So on occasion, there is no way to shade the canvas. Then I sometimes have to work on a sun-drenched canvas and find that I always paint the values too dark. I later adjust them in the studio. Once correct values are established, working in direct sun is not too bad. Sight-size cannot be applied to landscape paintings. I do always, though, place my easel so that the canvas is parallel to the scene I'm working on so that I can easily flick my eye from canvas to subject.

- Though blocking in an outdoor landscape painting is essentially the same as for a studio work, the sight-size method cannot truly be applied. Generally the area I intend to compose is vastly larger than my canvas, so my initial layout is usually revised as I break up the larger masses into smaller components. Some artists say drawing is not important in a landscape painting. I strongly disagree. I have used the analogy of a jigsaw puzzle in explaining the importance of drawing. If all the elements in a composition are not the right shape, the ensemble won't fit together.

▪ Another aspect of outdoor sketching in oil to which I try to respond is this: nature often presents me with a change in lighting or atmospheric effect that I think would make a more interesting painting than the effect I originally established. Once the elements in a finished sketch are established, they can be altered drastically and quickly: a higher key light effect can be applied over darker original values or vice versa.

▪ I lacked a definite grasp of Impressionist technique until reading a simple statement in Birge Harrison's book on landscape painting. Harrison said: "Colors dance, but values stay put." I suddenly perceived that the scintillating color effects I had enjoyed in Impressionist paintings were the result of a close understanding of the use of values within a given color area. Though the painter might juxtapose opposing hues in a sky, for example, each of the separate hues was carefully mixed with white on the palette so that their values were identical. With this revelation, I began applying broken-color technique in my paintings in an effort to enhance that vibration of color that is apparent in nature.

▪ Typically the sky is lighter than the light yellowish imprimatura pigment with which I usually tone my canvas. Working outdoors, I begin with the lights, sometimes painting the sky area a flat white in anticipation of seeing an interesting cloud effect. Any whites I intend to use in the land portion, I indicate at the start too. In recent years, I have used darker values in my darks than I once did; something I learned from the Hudson River School and Barbizon painters. I have recently done outdoor

Another view of Koestner studio, showing mirror at upper left, 2001.

paintings on a white canvas—something Monet also did in his late work.

▪ I try to get all the values (degrees of light and dark) as best I can, given pigment limitations.

▪ I have not given special attention to keeping my values to a set number, but I select what light gives me the most interesting pattern of values and best contrasts of light and dark. Sometimes, for example, I'll change a morning painting to afternoon because it would be more interesting light.

Composition

▪ To organize my paintings compositionally I have sometimes used the principles found in the book, *The Elements of Dynamic Symmetry*, by Jay Hambidge (Dover Publications, Inc., 1967). A rectangle created with this system—what the ancient Greeks termed the "golden section"—includes guidelines for placing important elements in the painting. (See diagram, above right, and basic explanation, below.)

The diagonal line from A (the midpoint of the base of the original square) to B is the radius of the arc B C. The vertical lines marking the overlapping two-inch squares are marked D and B. The smaller squares which also overlap are marked 1 and 2, and 3 and 4. Anywhere along the interior horizontal or vertical lines and their intersections are good places to position prominent elements of the composition. I have often used these golden section divisions in my paintings.

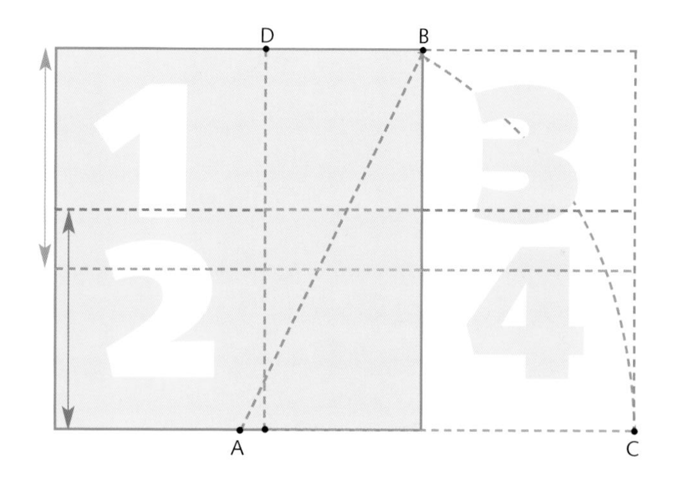

▪ A painting in the 1980s, *Lake Pepin* (page 81), was done mostly on one spot, but then I moved down the road to include a particular tree. I worked in three different spots to get the various elements I wanted in this picture. In our woods here, I've done parts of a picture in one location and parts in another.

▪ I use many different approaches in painting a landscape depending on the situation. In the painting, *Mississippi Valley, Autumn* (page 22), I never completed the color sketch but worked from pencil sketches and notes done at the scene. I recently found a small tracing paper diagram of my proposed composition (on a grid), from which I got my drawing onto the canvas. In all studio landscapes done from color sketches and photos, I draw the elements of the composition in pencil on the canvas. On works done locally, I generally stick pretty close to transcribing what nature offers me. I usually use a number four bright (bristle) brush that gives me a fine line to block in the composition, using mostly a thin blue and white paint.

Hand-ground paint

▪ Originally I chose to grind my paints because I wanted faster drying paint than the commercial variety. I began the practice in 1949 while still a student at the Minneapolis School of Art, persuading the director to order pigments from New York so that I could buy them from the school supply store with my G.I. Bill money. Pigments were dirt cheap at that time. White lead was sixty cents a pound; now it is twenty dollars a pound. So it was cheaper to make my own paints. I also learned that commercial paints (though better in general then, than now) contained fillers like chalk to make up one-fourth to one-third of the tube volume. I soon found that I used quite a bit less paint to achieve a desired tone with white than was necessary with commercial paint. Today the Old Holland Brand Colors are equal to my hand-ground product but very costly. I still have dry pigments so it is practical for me to continue making one half to two thirds of the paint I use. All the instruction for hand-grinding paints is contained in manuals such as Max Doerner's *The Materials of the Artist and Their Use in Painting*. Now I buy half my white paint (Old Holland brand, and mix that with a cup of hand-ground flake white) and a few infrequently used colors, but the bulk of the paint I use is hand ground. Paint that dries more quickly is still one reason for grinding my own, but I also get colors that are more intense. Nature has a glow that cannot be matched by paint, but the more intense my paint colors are, the better equipped I am to record what I see. There was once a cost advantage, too, which is no longer the case, but I've found that a tube of my paint lasts half again longer than the commercial product because it takes less to get the desired tints. The biggest drawback for anyone who might want to start hand-grinding now is the difficulty of obtaining good cold-pressed linseed oil (the best vehicle for grinding colors), and the high cost of pigments today.

▪ In addition to some Old Holland Paints, I use a Windsor and Newton emerald green called Windsor Emerald.

▪ Since 1949 I have primarily used Maroger's medium to thin, when necessary, a paint I will apply to my canvas. The medium consists of combining one-half mastic varnish with one-half "black oil." The mastic varnish is made by melting mastic crystals in pure gum spirits of turpentine—one part crystals to two parts turpentine. The black oil is made by combining cold-pressed linseed oil with litharge (a lead-derivative pigment). I usually use about one ounce litharge to sixteen ounces of the oil. This concoction is then boiled. Old manuscripts refer to cooking over a "low fire." I cook my oil on an electric hot plate, starting at low, slowly raising it to medium, and finally to high temperature over about an hour's time. The mixture should be stirred occasionally. About midway in the cooking process the oil becomes muddy looking. Maroger gives centigrade readings for various stages of the cooking. At about 150 degrees the litharge will agglutinate at the bottom of the receptacle. Toward 210 degrees the deposit softens and at about 230 degrees will finally mix with the oil. At this heat, the muddy appearance of the oil disappears and it becomes clear and the color of coffee. I have never used a thermometer but just monitored the various

Don Koestner grinding pigment in Hastings studio, 1985.

stages and have learned to turn off the heat before the oil fully clarifies and the litharge fully melts. The oil starts to smoke after 210 degrees and I avoid that. My oil, although brown when I take it off the heat, turns black when I cover the kettle. The kettle has to cool considerably before pouring the mixture into a bottle. The resulting medium is a brown jell that can be put on the palette like other pigments. This medium has been strongly denounced by many artists and material's texts as being "absolutely impermanent." However, I've used it for fifty-five years and my paintings are holding up quite well. For glazing I have used Taubes Copal Medium since the 1960s; it is no longer available but because of valued friends I have a lifetime supply.

▪ Turpentine has become a significant problem for me. Genuine turpentine is difficult to find. This makes it impossible to make mastic varnish which I use for my Maroger medium because mastic crystals dissolve only in genuine pure turpentine. I have bought several cans of turpentine labeled Pure Gum Spirits of Turpentine from Utrecht, K-Mart, and a paint store; Kirk Richard also sent me two ounces of English Distilled Turpentine which he uses in his medium, but none of these will dissolve my mastic crystals! But I have recently been able to purchase some mastic varnish from Kremer Pigments (a German firm with a New York office), so I can once again make Maroger medium. I still use Taubes Copal Medium for glazing.

▪ I still have some commercially prepared Fredrix canvas which I'm slowly using up for sketching canvases. But for the past six or seven years I've been buying rolls of unprimed canvas and putting my own ground on them; a practice I pursued in my early years also. Most commercially grounded canvas today has too much oil in it so it can be rolled up tightly without cracking. Such canvas is almost completely non-absorbent, often having a shiny gloss. As I've been using some heavier pigment surfaces lately, I want a semi-absorbent ground to which the paint can adhere strongly. Again, I have turned to Doerner and use his recipe for a half-chalk ground: use one third rabbit-skin glue liquid, one third titanium white pigment and one third chalk; to this warmed mixture about one fourth measure of boiled linseed oil is slowly dripped and stirred well until an emulsion is formed. This is then brushed on the canvas which has previously been coated with a weak rabbit-skin glue gel, applied with a spatula. I usually apply two or three coats.

▪ I use glazing and scumbling. (Scumbling is putting light over dark and usually has white in it. Glazing is putting dark over light. Both are liquid but a scumble is more opaque.) In recalling a particular painting I had done years ago, I have difficulty saying whether or not it may have contained glazes or scumbling because both techniques are usually combined with direct painting and their effect is not that obvious. One relatively recent painting, *Morning Ground Fog* (page 88), combines much scumbling in the fog areas and glazing with vermillion over the orange trees on the right edge. In another

Wisconsin Valley Farm (color study), 1999, 16 x 20 in. (painting on page 71)

Autumn Asters (color study), 2000, 10 x 16 in. (painting on page 86)

older painting, *Rattlesnake Bluff* (page 108), I remember glazing barium chromate yellow over the sunlit portion of the bluff. Though put on as a glaze it had the effect of lightening the value so it worked essentially as a scumble. The entire painting, *The Lone Farm* (page 87), had a glaze of vermillion over the finished picture.

Production

- For painting purposes I haven't seen any area of the North Shore of Lake Superior that would make better painting subjects than our one-and-a-half acres. I have high views from thirty-foot cliffs and lake level views from our beach. The rocky islands off-shore provide centers of interest. The four seasons, the wide variety of atmospheric effects and the ever-changing lake allow me to paint very different works from the same spots. I've done more than a hundred paintings on the property; ten or more from various windows of the house.

- I have often painted away from northern Minnesota, my home since 1986, for three reasons. One is that the deciduous trees and farmlands of the Midwest still attract me, and offer color and shapes I don't encounter in the northland. The second is that I have discovered I can extend my autumn painting by going south a bit. I have brought back fall sketches from Missouri, the Blue Ridge Mountains, West Virginia, Iowa, Illinois, and Wisconsin. And, third, I like to go into the winter with material I can utilize to produce landscapes in the studio. I make oil sketches on such trips, taking along a number of small canvases of varying shapes. If possible, I spend as many as five or six sessions on a sketch so I can pretty much rely on them for translating to larger works. If time allows (it usually doesn't) I also make a pencil drawing to pin down shapes more accurately.

- Fern generally accompanied me on fall painting trips, and took photos of my landscape subjects while I was sketching. They have been useful for some aspects of the drawing. Locally, I avoid their use entirely. In fact, I have not bothered to learn the operation of the camera, and when out alone never carried one until after Fern's death. Unfortunately, people today, having not observed much themselves, accept the photograph as a true transcript of nature. In regard to color and value, a photograph certainly is not, and it also flattens perspective. I'm adamantly against the painter making much use of photography.

▪ In my early years, and up through my fifties I often worked on three paintings a day—morning, afternoon, and evening. I preferred the evening light as I could work toward my effect. In the morning I had to work away from the early light I wanted. In recent years, I work outdoors on only one three- or four-hour sketch or painting per day. In the studio, during the winter, I work two hours in the morning and several hours in the afternoon. When we made fall trips, Fern and I would bring home four, or as many as six, oil sketches and I would work on that many larger canvases alternately during the winter. Earlier, I painted outside in the winter and also worked on still lifes. Since the early 1950s I have painted more than 2,000 pictures.

—Notes compiled by Annette LeSueur

Adjusting umbrella, North Shore, 1997.